PowerKids Readers:
Nature Books™

Mountains

Jacqueline Dwyer

The Rosen Publishing Group's
PowerKids Press™
New York

To Tom

Published in 2001 by The Rosen Publishing Group, Inc.
29 East 21st Street, New York, NY 10010

Copyright © 2001 by The Rosen Publishing Group, Inc.

First Edition

Book Design: Michael de Guzman
Layout: Felicity Erwin and Edwin Yoo

Photo Credits: p. 1 © F.P.G./Gary Randall; p. 5 © International Stock/Orion; p. 7 © F.P.G./Lee Foster; p. 9 © CORBIS/Galen Rowell; p. 11 © CORBIS/Kennen Ward; p. 13 © F.P.G./John Terence Turner; p. 15 © F.P.G./Charles Benes; p. 17 © CORBIS/W. Wayne Lockwood, M.D.; p. 19 © F.P.G./Sanford Schulwolf; p. 21 © CORBIS/Karl Weatherly; p. 22 (volcano) © International Stock/Warren Faidley.

Dwyer, Jackie, 1970–
    Mountains / by Jacqueline Dwyer. — 1st ed.
        p.cm. — (PowerKids readers. Nature books)
    Summary: Describes different kinds of mountains, some of the animals that live on them, and how people use mountains in various ways.
    ISBN: 0-8239-5680-6 (lib. bdg. : alk. paper)
    1. Mountains—Juvenile literature. [1. Mountains.]I. Title. II. Series.

GB512 .D98 2000
551.43'2—dc21

                                                                                    99-055187

Manufactured in the United States of America

2

Contents

Mountains are very high hills.

5

Most mountains are near other mountains. They form a row of mountains. A long row of mountains is called a mountain range.

There are mountains all over the world. Mount Everest is the highest mountain in the world.

9

A volcano is a special
kind of mountain.
Sometimes hot lava pours
out of a volcano.

11

It can snow a lot on a mountain. Sometimes there can be too much snow on a mountain. The heavy snow slides down the mountain. This is called an avalanche.

It is windy at the top of a tall mountain. The wind bends the trees that grow near the top of a mountain.

15

There are many animals that live on mountains. Mountain sheep are animals that live on mountains.

17

Some mountains have snow on them in the summer. People like to hike up snowy mountains. Dogs like to hike up snowy mountains, too.

In the winter, people like to visit the mountains covered in snow. It is fun to ski down a snowy mountain.

21

Words to Know

AVALANCHE

HIKE

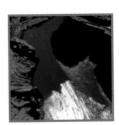
LAVA

MOUNTAINS

MOUNTAIN
SHEEP

SKI

VOLCANO

22

Here are more books to read about mountains:

Mountains (Exploring Our World)
by Terry Jennings
Marshall Cavendish

Hills and Mountains (Young Explorer)
by Mark C. W. Sleep
Wayland Publishers Limited

To learn more about mountains, check out this Web site:
http://encarta.msn.com/find/search.asp?z=1&pg=1&search=mountains

23

Index

Word Count: 173

Note to Librarians, Teachers, and Parents

PowerKids Readers (Nature Books) are specially designed to help emergent and beginning readers build their skills in reading for information. Simple vocabulary and concepts are paired with photographs of real kids in real-life situations or stunning, detailed images from the natural world around them. Readers will respond to written language by linking meaning with their own everyday experiences and observations. Sentences are short and simple, employing a basic vocabulary of sight words, as well as new words that describe objects or processes that take place in the natural world. Large type, clean design, and photographs corresponding directly to the text all help children to decipher meaning. Features such as a contents page, picture glossary, and index help children get the most out of PowerKids Readers. They also introduce children to the basic elements of a book, which they will encounter in their future reading experiences. Lists of related books and Web sites encourage kids to explore other sources and to continue the process of learning.

Impact

Impact

James C. Dekker

orca soundings

ORCA BOOK PUBLISHERS

Library and Archives Canada Cataloguing in Publication

Dekker, James C
Impact / written by James C. Dekker.

(Orca soundings)
ISBN 978-1-55143-995-2 (pbk.).--ISBN 978-1-55143-997-6 (bound)

I. Title. II. Series: Orca soundings

PS8607.E4825I46 2009   jC813'.6   C2009-900015-6

Summary: After the brutal murder of their son and brother, family
members read their victim impact statements in court.

First published in the United States, 2009
Library of Congress Control Number: 2008943718

Orca Book Publishers gratefully acknowledges the support for its publishing
programs provided by the following agencies: the Government of Canada
through the Book Publishing Industry Development Program and the Canada
Council for the Arts, and the Province of British Columbia through the BC
Arts Council and the Book Publishing Tax Credit.

Cover design by Teresa Bubela
Cover photography by Getty Images

Orca Book Publishers   Orca Book Publishers
PO Box 5626, Stn. B   PO Box 468
Victoria, BC Canada   Custer, WA USA
V8R 6S4   98240-0468

www.orcabook.com
Printed and bound in Canada.
Printed on 100% PCW recycled paper.
12 11 10 09 • 4 3 2 1

To Mom

Chapter One

"When I was sixteen," my father says, his voice trembling, "my younger brother died. He was eleven years old. It was an accident. He ran out into the road—he was chasing a ball. He got hit by a car. My parents were devastated. And I remember my mother saying to me that the worst pain in the world is the pain of a parent who has just lost a child."

My father is a big man. I don't mean he's fat. He isn't. I mean he's taller than most people, except maybe professional basketball players. He's strong. He's tough. At least, that's what I always thought. But there he is, his head down, looking at the papers in his hand. The papers are filled with words he has written. His voice almost breaks as he reads what is on those papers. He is big, but he looks small and tired and beaten down.

"Now I know what my mother meant," he says. "I have been living with this knowledge for two years."

Two years ago, when I was sixteen, my father lost a child. Two years ago, my brother Mark died. He was seventeen—exactly one year, one month and one day older than me.

It happened the first week in October. Mark had a part-time job at a fast-food restaurant. He worked every weekend, but he also had to work until midnight once during the week, every week, even though his manager knew he had school the next day. It happened on one of those nights.

Mark called home before he left the restaurant. I was in my room. I was supposed to be asleep, but I was watching a movie on my computer. I heard the phone. I knew it was Mark. He hated making those calls, but my mother insisted. He called and said he was just leaving, that he was making one stop on the way to pick up a sandwich, and that he would be home in forty-five minutes at the latest. I heard my mother say he didn't have to buy a sandwich. She would make one for him. For some reason, my mother thought it was a waste of money to buy stuff like sandwiches and burgers, things she could make at home.

An hour later, when my movie was over, I heard my mother go downstairs. I knew right away why. Mark wasn't home yet. I went down too. I said, "You worry too much, Mom."

She told me to go back to bed. "It's a school day tomorrow," she said. Then she went to the front door, looked out through the little window in it and said, "He should have been home by now."

"Maybe he missed the bus," I said. "Maybe he had to wait for the next one."

10

The buses don't run as often late at night as they do during the day.

"If he had to wait for the next bus, then he should be home in fifteen minutes," my mother said. "Go to bed, Jordan."

I went upstairs, but I didn't fall asleep. I lay in bed and waited to hear the front door open.

Fifteen minutes passed.

Twenty minutes.

Half an hour.

I heard my mother come up the stairs and go into her room, which is next to mine. I heard her say to my father, "I'm worried. Mark is late. He's not answering his phone."

I heard my father say, "I'm sure he's fine. Maybe he missed his bus."

"He should have been home forty-five minutes ago," my mother said. "He hasn't called, and I can't get hold of him."

A few minutes later I heard my parents go downstairs. I got out of bed and followed them. My father was dressed. He had his car keys in his hand. He looked worried, but when

I asked him if everything was okay, he said, "I'm sure it is. But you know your mother. I'm going to go and see if I can find Mark."

My mother stood at the door and looked out the window the whole time he was gone.

The next part I know only because I heard it told so many times.

My father got in the car and drove along the bus route to the fast-food place where Mark worked. He drove almost all the way to the restaurant.

Three blocks from the restaurant and two blocks from the bus stop, right in front of a nearly empty parking lot, he saw flashing lights. They turned out to be from an ambulance and a couple of police cars. There were a few other cars there too, which turned out to belong to some detectives.

My father said it never occurred to him that all those flashing lights could have anything to do with him. He drove two more blocks to the restaurant, which by then was closed. There was no sign of Mark. So he turned the car around and started to go back the way he had come. This time, he said, he turned his head when he passed all those police cars. He saw now that there was a body in the parking lot. It was covered up, and there was something lying nearby. He couldn't see who it was or even if it was a man or a woman. He just saw it was a body. He drove right by and kept driving.

He said he was maybe ten blocks away before he suddenly realized what it was that he had seen lying near the body. It was a paper bag from a sandwich place. He said he recognized it because it was the sandwich place that Mark always liked to go to. He said everything moved in slow motion after that, like when you're having a nightmare and you're running as fast as you can, but it seems like you're hardly moving at all and whatever is after you is gaining on you until you know it's going to catch you. That's when you scream. That's when you wake up.

But my father didn't wake up. He couldn't. He wasn't asleep. But that didn't mean he wasn't having a nightmare.

He drove back to where he had seen the flashing lights.

He parked the car.

He went up to a uniformed police officer who was guarding the area where the body was, in a body bag now.

He said that as he approached that cop, he thought Mark would have a good laugh if he knew what his old man was about to do. But he did it anyway. He said to the cop, "Excuse me, I'm sorry to bother you. My name is Drew Spencer. My son is late coming home. He works right over there." He pointed across the street to the fast-food restaurant. "He's seventeen years old, brown hair, brown eyes. His name is Mark Spencer."

He said he saw something in the cop's eyes as soon as he said Mark's name.

He said the cop told him, "Wait here, please, sir." The cop went over to a man in a suit and an overcoat. He said something to the man, and the man came over to where my father was waiting.

The man said, "Mr. Spencer? I'm Detective Carlin." Detective Carlin paused for a second before he added, "Homicide."

Chapter Two

"Mark was my firstborn son," my father says, reading the words he has written. "He was a good boy and a hard worker. His mother and I were so proud of him."

But that didn't stop someone from killing him.

The police said Mark had been beaten to death. My parents saw him afterward, after they took his body away. They saw what had been done to him. I only heard about it.

The way the police pieced it together, it happened something like this:

Mark called my mother almost exactly at midnight to tell her that he was just leaving the fast-food place where he worked. Mark had been on shift with two other people that night—an eighteen-year-old guy who handled all the cooking, and a nineteen-year-old girl who was the shift manager for the night.

The way it was supposed to work, at least two people had to be in the restaurant until the place was locked for the night. The cook left first, at a quarter to twelve, after the last of everything had been cooked and the kitchen cleaned. There were no customers in the place when he left, just Mark and the shift manager.

The shift manager's boyfriend was waiting for her, so she asked Mark if he would mind locking up, even though it was against company policy for her to leave him there alone. Mark said, "No problem."

The shift manager said she left at ten minutes to twelve. The police assume—but don't know for sure—that Mark stayed until midnight. He called my mother, he locked

up the place and he walked two blocks to
the sandwich shop, where the lone employee
remembered him coming in and ordering a
sandwich to go. The sandwich shop employee
said he thinks Mark came into the place at
six or seven minutes past midnight and left
four or five minutes later. He said he didn't
remember seeing anyone else on the street
outside the sandwich shop. He remembered
a couple of taxis going by, but that's it.

At twelve twenty or thereabouts, a taxi
drove past the parking lot where Mark was
found. The driver said he saw people in the
parking lot. He thought there were maybe
four or five of them and they were all guys,
but he wasn't sure. He said it looked like
one of the people was acting "in a menacing
fashion." But he said he couldn't stop because
he was on his way to pick up a fare.

Around twelve thirty, a pizza delivery guy
stopped across the street from the parking
lot and rang the buzzer of an apartment that
was located above a video store opposite
the parking lot. He was buzzed in, went up,
delivered the pizza, collected what he was

owed, plus a tip, and went back down to the street again. He said he was just getting into his car when he heard what sounded like a groan. He said it was coming from the parking lot across the street. He went to investigate. He said he saw people in the parking lot, but he couldn't make them out clearly at first. He heard the groan again, and he called out, "Is everything okay over there?"

Right away, he said, the people ran. He said he was sure there were four of them. He said three of them ran right under a streetlight and he got a pretty good look at them. He said that seeing them run like that made him think that something was wrong, so he went into the parking lot to take a look. That's when he found out where the groaning was coming from—from a young man who was bleeding and who looked like he had been badly beaten.

The pizza delivery guy used his cell phone to call 9-1-1. He said he tried to help the young man, but he didn't know what to do. He said the young man said one word to him: *Tony*. He said by the time anyone showed up, it looked to him like the young man had stopped breathing.

The young man was Mark.

The police asked my parents if they knew anyone named Tony. They didn't.

They asked me the same question. I went cold all over. I said they should talk to Shannon.

"Who's Shannon?" the cops said.

"She's a girl Mark was seeing. I heard someone say she used to go with a guy named Tony."

The police talked to Shannon next. Shannon went to the same school as Mark and me, which is how I know what happened when the police talked to her. All the girls at school were talking about it after it happened.

The police asked Shannon if she knew anyone named Tony. One of the girls at my school said that Shannon's face went white when they asked her that. She told the police that her ex-boyfriend's name was Tony. Tony Lofredo. He didn't go to our school. In fact, Shannon said, she had transferred to our school after she broke up with Tony. She told the police that Tony was the jealous type and that he wouldn't leave her alone. That's why she had changed schools. She described Tony to the police, and her description matched the description of one of the people that the pizza delivery guy had seen running out of the parking lot.

When my father heard that, I think he thought it would all go pretty fast. He thought the police would arrest Tony, and Tony would tell them who else had been with him. Then they'd go to court and that would be that.

Of course, it didn't happen that way. And it sure didn't happen fast.

Chapter Three

"People thought highly of Mark," my father says, standing up there in front of everyone, his hands trembling now as he continues to read without looking up. "His teachers liked him. His boss where he worked and his coworkers all liked him. The church was full for his funeral."

The church *was* full for Mark's funeral. All my relatives were there. Our neighbors were there, even the Mercers and their son Kyle, who lived two doors up from us. Kyle looked down at the ground most of the time.

All Mark's friends were there. So were his coworkers. Shannon was there, even though she had only gone out with Mark a couple of times. There were a whole bunch of girls with her, pressing in close to her, like if they didn't, she would fall over from grief. She cried a lot for someone who didn't know Mark all that well.

My mother cried through the whole service too. My father sat beside her, holding her hand and looking straight ahead. He didn't cry, but I bet he wanted to. I know I did.

After the funeral, everything was a blur for a while. My parents were a mess. My mother could hardly get up off the couch, but the house was filled with food. People kept bringing over casseroles and salads and pies. The house was full of crying too. Some days I'd get home from school and there would be my mother, crying in the kitchen, one of her friends with her, handing her tissue after tissue and listening to her weep.

My father talked to the police a lot. One time I heard him yelling into the phone that they knew it was this boy Tony, why didn't they just go ahead and arrest him? I guess he didn't like whatever the answer was because he slammed down the receiver and stormed out of the house. I don't know when he came back, but it was long after I'd gone to bed. I found him sprawled on the couch the next morning. My mother called the plant and told them that my father wouldn't be in to work that day.

My mother cried all day, but my father mostly went to work, and I went to school. It was the last place I wanted to be, but I went anyway. I thought at first that it would be better than being at home and listening to my mother cry all the time. But it wasn't. I have some good friends. They tried to do the right thing. They showed up to the funeral. They said they were sorry about what had happened to Mark. They said I must really miss him. But after the first couple of days, well, it wasn't *their* brother. If they thought about it, they could kind of imagine what I felt like. But they didn't think about it, not every minute of every day like I did. Why should they? They for sure didn't find themselves slamming their fist into a wall like I did a couple of times. They didn't all of a sudden start to cry in the middle of a basketball game like I did. Mark was good at basketball. We used to shoot hoops out in the driveway, just the two of us. But there I was a few weeks after it happened, shooting hoops with my friends. One minute I was scooping the ball and shooting it. The next minute I was seeing Mark. And right after that I was crying. If you want to freak out a bunch of guys, stand in the middle of the basketball court holding the ball and cry. Trust me, that'll do it.

One day when I got home after school, my father was getting out of the car in the driveway. Right away I knew something was up. My father was on the day shift that week. He didn't usually get home until at least a half hour after I did. But here he was, thirty minutes ahead of schedule, getting out of the car.

"Did you get off early?" I said.

"Something like that," he said. But I could tell by the look on his face that it wasn't anything like that at all.

I followed him into the house. He went straight through to the kitchen without taking off his work boots. That was another clue that something was going on. My father always took his boots off at the door. My mother insisted on it.

My mother was in the kitchen. I think she'd gone in there to start supper, but she wasn't cooking. She was standing at the kitchen sink, looking out the window into the backyard. She didn't seem to notice when my father and I came into the kitchen. She didn't turn around until my father went to her and put his hands on her shoulders and turned her around. Neither of us was surprised when we saw how red her eyes were and how wet her cheeks were.

"I talked to that police detective today," my father said quietly. "They've made some arrests, Sara. They've arrested four boys for what happened to Mark."

My mother stared blankly at him. It was

hard to tell if she understood what he was saying.

I felt my whole body tense up.

"Was one of them Tony Lofredo?" I asked.

My father nodded. "Tony Lofredo and two of his friends."

Tears were streaming down my mother's face, but I couldn't tell if she was crying because she was glad that, finally, the police had arrested someone or because what my father had just told her was making her remember all over again what had happened to Mark. She pressed up against my father, and he wrapped his arms around her.

I thought about what my father had just said. "Tony Lofredo and *two* of his friends?" I said. "But you said the police arrested four people. Tony and his two friends—that only makes three."

My father turned to look at me. "The fourth boy," he said in a quiet voice. "It's Kyle Mercer."

I felt sicker inside than I had ever felt.

Chapter Four

"When we heard that the police had arrested the people who killed our son, we thought it would ease our pain. But it didn't," my father says, reading. He looks up for the first time. He looks at my mother. I glance at her too. Her eyes are filled with tears, but she holds her head high.

It was crazy at our house for the first day or two after the police arrested Tony Lofredo, his two friends—whose names were Joey Karagiannis and Robert Teale—and Kyle Mercer. The media phoned—newspaper, radio, TV—and showed up at our door. They wanted to know what my parents thought about the arrests. They even asked me what I thought. After the first two days, my father unplugged the phone. He said anyone who needed to get in touch with him could call him on his cell phone. My father only gives out his cell phone number to close friends and to relatives.

Kyle Mercer went to the same school as me, so I couldn't get away from it there. Everyone was talking about what had happened. But it died down again fast, because after Kyle was arrested, they kept him locked up until the trial. They kept all four of them locked up.

Shannon disappeared from school. Someone said that her parents had decided to send her to a private school so she could get away from all the bad memories. At first that didn't make sense to me. She hadn't known Mark all that long. Then someone else told me that she had transferred because she felt guilty. She thought that if she had never gone out with Mark, he would still be alive. Maybe that was true.

After a week had passed, all the excitement died down. I thought the trial would happen a couple of weeks or maybe a couple of months later. Was I ever wrong!

A date was set for a preliminary inquiry. It got pushed back and pushed back. In the meantime, we were supposed to get on with our lives.

The worst Christmas of my life came and went. My father didn't go out and buy a Christmas tree the way he usually did. My mother didn't make batches and batches of Christmas cookies the way she usually did. Neither of them did any Christmas shopping. They gave me money and told me I should treat myself to whatever I wanted, but I couldn't think of anything.

The new year came, and still nothing happened. I had trouble concentrating on my schoolwork. Basically, I just didn't care. I failed every subject but math, and I got a D in that.

My mother, who had a part-time job at a store, spent more and more of her time in bed. After a while, she stopped going to work. They fired her. One of my aunts finally took her to the doctor. She was diagnosed with depression, and the doctor put her on medication. As far as I could see, it didn't do much good. The same aunt, who was single and a registered nurse, moved in with us to look after my mother.

My father went to work every day—at least, I think he did. But he didn't come home every night. A few times when he didn't show up, my aunt called the police. The first time she called them, my aunt and I were up all night, worried about what had happened to him. The police brought him home first thing the next morning, right after they found him. He had passed out at Mark's grave, an empty bottle of scotch beside him. The next couple of times he didn't come home, she called the police again. But every time they found him in the same place. So after a while, she stopped calling them. Instead she would wake me up, if I were asleep, which mostly, at night, I wasn't, and we would drive out to the cemetery together, load my father into the back of the car and bring him home. My aunt said it was a miracle that he managed to hang on to his job.

The street I live on is small—just two blocks long—and out of the way. It's a dead-end street where everyone knows everyone else because most people have lived there for a while and most people's kids play with most other people's kids and go to the same schools. It's the kind of street where, in summertime, everyone is out on their front porches or fooling around in their gardens or messing around with their tiny front lawns. People call across the street to each other. They wander up and down the street to gossip and exchange news. There's an annual beginning-of-summer street party. There's also an annual yard sale that everyone on the street participates in. "Everyone" includes my parents and Kyle Mercer's parents. Kyle's parents used to come over sometimes for beers and a barbecue—my father loved to invite the neighbors over, and everybody would sit out back and talk and listen to music and dance on a long, hot summer night. Mark and I were never super-close to Kyle, but he used to hang out with us when we were young. All the kids on the street hung out together. When Kyle started to spend time with guys who were bad news, my mother listened to his mother complain about it. She told Kyle's mother it was probably just a phase. She said good parents raise good boys, and she was sure Kyle was going to be just fine.

At first people on the street said they didn't blame Kyle's parents for what had happened. But when it was finally time for the first beginning-of-summer street party since Mark had died, it looked like things had changed. Both my parents went to the party, although neither of them wanted to. My father had started going to AA meetings by then, mostly because my aunt was dragging him to them, and he didn't want to go to a party where everyone would be drinking. My mother wanted to stay in bed. But my aunt made her get up and get dressed and even put a little makeup on. She made me go too.

One by one, people went up to my parents. It was as if my parents had just come back from a long trip, which, in a way, they had. They hadn't had much to do with the neighbors in months and months. People came and talked to them and hugged my mother. Then someone looked up the street at the Mercers' house. Soon everyone stopped talking and looked at the house too. Everyone seemed tense.

Mr. and Mrs. Mercer had just come out onto their porch. They looked over at the party. Mr. Mercer had a case of beer in his hands. Mrs. Mercer was carrying a big tray covered with plastic wrap—food for the party.

They looked down where everyone was gathered around my parents. Mrs. Mercer looked at Mr. Mercer. She shook her head. He said something to her, but she shook her head again and went back into the house. After a few minutes, he followed her inside. Everybody seemed to relax again.

A month later, a For Sale sign went up on the Mercers' front lawn. By the end of the summer, they were gone.

Chapter Five

"It has been so hard," my father says. He finishes the page he has been reading and shuffles it to the bottom of the small pile of sheets he is holding. I can't believe he has written so much. My father works on an assembly line. He reads the newspaper, mainly the sports page, but I have never seen him read a book. I have never seen him write anything but a check. "We have been here for every single day of this trial. We have heard everything that was said."

The trial started in January, nearly fifteen months after Mark was killed. In that time, my father stopped drinking, started again and then stopped again. By the first day of the trial, he had been sober for four straight months.

My mother stayed on antidepressants, but she didn't stay in bed. She got up and found another job at another store, a 24-hour grocery store this time. My aunt moved back to her own place.

All my friends graduated the spring before the trial started. I got a part-time job that fall and started taking classes at night to get my high school diploma. The plan was that I should be able to graduate by the Christmas after the trial.

My father arranged to work permanent nights at the plant so that he could attend the trial every day. My mother also worked it out so that if she was scheduled to work during the week, it would either be in the evening or at night. She didn't want to miss a single day either.

I tried to get my boss to scale my time back to Friday nights and Saturdays, but he said he needed me to work during the week. So I quit and got another job delivering pizza at night instead. We were all tired, but we all showed up every single day.

A real trial isn't like a trial on TV or in the movies. When you see a trial on TV, it seems like people are up there testifying for five or ten minutes at the most. It also seems like the lawyers and the prosecutors are really smooth.

But in real life, it's not like that. In real life, people can be up there testifying for an hour or two hours or even longer. Some of the lawyers stumble and fumble and say *um* and *er*. And there are plenty of times when they're arguing over whether they can even show a certain piece of evidence or ask certain questions, so sometimes court gets adjourned early, and sometimes it takes a day or two for the judge to decide about whatever the lawyers are arguing about. So sometimes it's boring or frustrating or just seems like a big waste of time.

They had a pathologist up there who talked about how Mark died. He'd been kicked and beaten with fists and with a piece of pipe. There were bruises and cuts all over his body, plus some broken ribs. She said what killed him, though, was having his head kicked in with some steel-toed boots. My mother cried quietly when she heard that. My father just stared straight ahead.

They had the pizza guy up. The prosecutor took him through everything he had seen and done, and asked him about what Mark had said, which was just the one word, the name *Tony*.

Then the defense lawyers got into it. There were four of them, one for each defendant. They grilled the pizza guy like you wouldn't believe. First they wanted to know what the pizza guy had seen. He described again hearing a sound and calling out to see if everything was okay, and then going into the parking lot and seeing Mark lying there and three or four guys running away.

The lawyers wanted to know if the pizza guy had seen the three or four guys doing anything except running away. The pizza guy said he hadn't.

The lawyers said, "You say you saw three or four guys. Which was it, *three* or *four*?" The pizza guy said he only got a good look at three guys, but that he was sure he saw a fourth person out of the corner of his eye.

Each lawyer wanted to know if the pizza guy had seen *his* client. The pizza guy said he was positive he had seen Tony and Joey and Robert. He said he hadn't seen Kyle. The lawyers went on and on, asking him how he could be so sure what he saw when he didn't know any of the defendants and when it was the middle of the night. The pizza guy said they ran right under a streetlight.

Tony's lawyer wanted to know what Mark had said about Tony. When the pizza guy said that all Mark said was Tony's name, Tony's lawyer said that for all the pizza guy knew, Mark could have been trying to say that Tony had tried to help him. He said that for all the pizza guy knew, the guys he saw fleeing the parking lot could have been running away because they were afraid they would be accused of something. Tony's lawyer kept on and on, trying to make the jury think that the pizza guy hadn't seen anything that would prove that Tony even touched Mark.

I glanced at my father. He was staring straight ahead, but I could tell he was angry.

Kyle's lawyer was asking over and over again, "So you didn't actually see my client? So you have no way of knowing whether my client was even there?" I felt my father tense up beside me.

They had a bunch of experts. The first was a cop who found fingerprints on a piece of pipe that had been found in a garbage can in an alley a few blocks from the parking lot where Mark died. He said one of the fingerprints belonged to Tony. Tony's lawyer asked him if there were any other fingerprints on the piece of pipe. It turned out there were—lots of them. The lawyer asked if the cop knew whose prints they were. The cop didn't. The lawyer asked if there was any way to tell whether someone else, someone whose prints the cop hadn't identified, had handled the pipe after Tony. The cop said there wasn't. Tony's lawyer asked if there was any way to tell if someone had picked up the pipe after Tony had put it down and had used it to beat Mark. The cop said there wasn't.

My father tensed up beside me again.

Then a forensic scientist went up and testified that Mark's blood had been found on the pipe along with a couple of Mark's hairs. She also testified that blood had been found on one of Tony's boots and that it was Mark's blood. Blood had also been found on the soles of Joey's boots, and on the toe of one of Robert's Doc Martens. They hadn't found any blood on anything that belonged to Kyle.

The lawyers all asked pretty much the same thing: Was there blood on the ground where Mark was found? The forensic scientist said that there was. Was it possible that Tony and Joey and Robert could have got the blood on their shoes or boots when they went to help Mark? The forensic scientist said that it was possible. Was there blood on any clothing belonging to the defendants? No, there wasn't. Kyle's lawyer asked again if there was any blood on anything belonging to Kyle. The forensic scientist said no, there wasn't.

Another police officer testified, a homicide cop. He explained how the name Tony had led him to Shannon, and that had led him to Tony's school, where he got a photograph of Tony and found out who Tony's friends were. He then presented the pizza guy and the taxi driver with a photo array—a set of pictures that included Tony and a bunch of other guys who looked similar to him. He did the same thing with Joey and Robert and Kyle. The taxi guy couldn't recognize anyone, but the pizza guy picked out Tony and Joey and Robert right away.

The detective said that he spoke to each of the three and they all said the same thing— they were just hanging out that night and they didn't know Mark. The homicide detective said they were vague on where they were hanging out and they couldn't tell him a single place they had been where someone might have seen them and might remember them.

He got a search warrant and their houses were searched. That's how he got the shoes and boots. He said that if he had to guess, the defendants had gotten rid of their clothes but had just washed their boots and shoes. All of the lawyers objected to that, and the judge cautioned both the homicide cop and the prosecutor.

I started to worry. It all came down to the pizza guy. He had seen Tony and Joey and Robert. But he hadn't actually seen them do anything. What if they got off?

Chapter Six

"We have looked at the four young men who are accused of killing our son," my father reads. "We have looked at them and I can tell you, in all honesty, that there were times when I couldn't see any difference between them and our Mark. They look like ordinary boys."

Shannon was called to testify. She was pale and kept biting her lower lip, which is how I knew she was nervous. She looked at the prosecutor the whole time. He asked her about her relationship with Tony.

"He used to be my boyfriend," she said.

"For how long?"

"For two years," she said.

"And then what happened?"

"We broke up."

"Why did you break up?"

"Because if another guy even looked at me or spoke to me, even if he was just asking me what time it was, Tony would freak out. One time I was working on a school project with a guy who was assigned to work with me. We didn't have any choice, the teacher made the assignments. We were in the library together, just the two of us. Someone told Tony that we were there, and Tony came and beat the guy up."

Tony's lawyer objected.

"He did," Shannon said. "If you don't believe me, you can ask Michael Riordan. He was in the hospital for a week. He almost lost an eye."

The whole time she was saying that, Tony's lawyer was objecting.

The prosecutor asked Shannon if Tony had ever hurt her.

"He slapped me around a couple of times, yeah," she said. She kept her eyes on the prosecutor. Tony was looking at her the whole time she was up there.

"Can you tell the court why he did that?" the prosecutor said.

Tony's lawyer objected again. He said that Shannon couldn't read Tony's mind and couldn't testify as to what he was thinking.

The prosecutor said, "Shannon, can you tell the court what happened when Tony slapped you around?"

"It happened twice," Shannon said. "The first time, Tony wanted me to go out with him on Saturday night. We always spent Saturday night together. But I said I couldn't because I had to go to my grandparents' anniversary party. He wanted to go with me, but I said he couldn't. My parents didn't like Tony. They didn't want him at the party. But I didn't tell Tony that because I knew it would make him mad. I just told him that it was a family-only party, so he couldn't come. Then he told me

I shouldn't go either. When I said I had to, he hit me."

"How did he hit you?"

"He slapped me across the face. Twice. Hard."

"What about the second time?"

"The second time, I told him I was too tired to go out with him. By then I wasn't sure if I wanted to see him anymore. This was after he beat up Michael Riordan."

Tony's lawyer objected again.

"Tony argued with me. He said he really wanted to see me. He said he'd had a tough week and he wanted to have some fun. When I told him again I was too tired, he punched me in the face. I ended up with a black eye. My parents wanted me to report him to the police, but I was afraid to. So instead they made me transfer to another school."

"How did Tony react to that?"

"He didn't like it," Shannon said. "He called me all the time. He left messages. He showed up at my new school. He'd be waiting for me at the end of the day. He said he wanted me back, and he'd get mad at me when I told him it was over."

"How did you meet Mark Spencer?" the prosecutor asked.

I held my breath.

"Mark went to the school I transferred to," Shannon said. "I noticed him right away. Mark was good-looking. He was nice too. I heard people talking about him all the time."

She glanced at where my mother and father and I were sitting. She looked at my parents. I held my breath again. She didn't look at me.

"Mark asked me out," she said. "We went out a couple of times. He was nice."

"Did Tony ever see you with Mark Spencer?" the prosecutor asked.

"Yes," Shannon said. "One time we came out of school together. Mark must have said something funny, because I remember I was laughing. Then I saw Tony. He came up to me and demanded to know who Mark was. I told him it was none of his business. He tried to grab me, but Mark shoved him away. I think Tony would have done something, but a cop car went by, and I could see the cops were looking at what was happening. So Tony took off."

"When did this happen?"

"About a week before Mark…before he died."

"Did Tony do anything that led you to believe that he might want to hurt Mark?"

"He phoned me. He wanted to know who Mark was. He wanted to know his name. But I didn't tell him."

"Did he say why he wanted to know Mark's name?"

"He said he wanted to talk to him."

"Why didn't you tell him who Mark was?"

"I was afraid he wanted to hurt Mark the way he hurt Michael Riordan."

Tony's lawyer asked Shannon a lot of questions about her and Tony.

He asked why Shannon had stayed with Tony for two whole years. Shannon said that he was nice at first.

The lawyer asked her about a party she and Tony went to just before Shannon transferred schools. He asked her if it was true that she got mad at Tony because he was flirting with another girl. She said no. He asked her if she knew there were several witnesses he could produce who would testify that she had told them she was mad at Tony because he was flirting with this girl and she was going to get even with him if it was the last thing she did. She said no, but I could tell that some of the jurors were wondering if she was telling the truth.

Then Tony's lawyer asked if that's what she was doing now—getting even with Tony. She said no. He asked her if that was the real reason she transferred schools—because she couldn't stand seeing Tony with another girl. She said no. He asked her if anyone had seen Tony give her that black eye. She said no. He asked her if she was sure she hadn't given herself that black eye and then blamed Tony for it, as a way of getting even with him. He asked if that was the real reason she hadn't reported Tony to the police—because he hadn't hit her at all.

Shannon's face was red by then. She

said no. She said she would never do anything like that. She said everything she said about Tony was the truth. She said—

"No more questions," Tony's lawyer said.

Chapter Seven

"We worried about our younger son, Jordan,"
my father reads. I wait, but he does not look
at me the way he looked at my mother earlier.
"We know what a terrible toll his brother's
death has taken on him."

Michael Riordan was called as a witness. He
said what Shannon had already described.
He said that Tony Lofredo had come into
the school library when he was working on

a project with Shannon. Tony pulled him up out of his chair and punched him in the stomach and said that would teach him to fool around with Shannon. Michael said that Tony then punched him in the face, and he kept punching him. He said Tony got suspended, but even then he was afraid to go back to school because Tony used to hang around across the street. He said he transferred schools to get away from Tony. He said he made sure he didn't transfer to the same school as Shannon because he didn't want Tony to get the wrong idea.

Tony's lawyer objected.

That afternoon, after court was recessed for the day and I was outside, waiting for my parents, who had stayed behind to talk to the prosecutor, Shannon came out onto the sidewalk. She was pretty when she was at my school, but that had been almost two years ago. She was even prettier now. I guess I was staring at her, because she smiled at me as she walked toward me.

"You're Mark's brother," she said. "It's Jason, right?"

I felt my cheeks burn the way they always did when I was embarrassed.

"Jordan," I said.

"Right," she said. She smiled at me the way you smile at some stranger your parents have just introduced you to. "Well," she said. She paused, as if she wasn't sure what to say next. A car horn tooted and she turned her head toward the sound. A look of relief flooded her face. "I have to go," she said. "My boyfr—" Her cheeks turned red. "My ride is here."

She ran to a car that had pulled up at the curb. She got inside. The driver leaned over and kissed her on the cheek. He looked a couple of years older than me. I watched his car pull away from the curb. I watched Shannon disappear.

Seeing Shannon made me realize how much had changed since Mark had died. It also took me back, way back—to school the way it used to be when I actually cared about it, to what it was like being the kid brother of one of the most popular guys in my school, to how things were always so easy for Mark when they were so hard for me. Back to when I used to wish I was more like Mark. I wanted to be as outgoing as he was, as confident, as comfortable around people. But I wasn't.

The new girl at my school was a good example. I noticed her the very first day of school, which was just a couple of months before Mark died. She sat two rows over and one seat up from me in homeroom, but she wasn't in any of my classes. Her locker was down the hall from mine. She was quiet the first couple of days, but after that she made friends with some girls. I used to see her swinging down the hall with them, laughing and enjoying herself. I wondered what she would say if I asked her out. I wondered if she would turn me down or, worse, laugh at me. A girl I'd known my whole life, but who I wasn't interested in and who wasn't interested in me, told me that the new girl used to go out with a guy at her old school but they had broken up. I still didn't ask her out. The truth was I had never asked a girl out before. Besides, I hadn't even talked to her yet. If I'd been Mark instead of me, I wouldn't have hesitated for even a second. I would have asked her out, just like that. And she would have said yes, just like that.

But I wasn't Mark.

I started to sweat every time I saw her.

It was the third week of school before I got up the nerve to say something to her. She was at her locker one morning. It was early, so the hallway was almost deserted. She had unlocked her locker but was having trouble getting it open. That happened sometimes—kids fooled around in the halls and slammed each other into the lockers. Sometimes the lockers got dented, and that made them hard to open. When I saw she was having trouble, I asked her if she needed some help.

"If you don't mind," she said.

I had to put a lot of effort into it, but I finally got it open.

"You should talk to one of the janitors and ask him to fix it," I said. "Or talk to Mr. Moorcock." He was our homeroom teacher.

"Thanks," she said. "I'll do that."
She started to get stuff out of her locker.
I watched her and tried to think of something
to say. Then two of the girls she had started
hanging out with showed up. They totally
ignored me, so I went back to my locker.
My heart was pounding in my chest. I should
have said something else. I shouldn't have
frozen up.

I watched her for the rest of the week,
waiting for a chance to talk to her alone. The
same girl who had told me that the new girl
didn't have a boyfriend also told me that she
liked football, so I planned to ask her if she
was going to the game that was coming up. It
was the next week before I finally spotted her
without a whole bunch of other girls around.

She was at her locker again, only this time
it was after school. There was no one else
around. I walked over to her. I tried to make
it look casual.

"Hi," I said.

She was taking books out of her locker
and loading them into a backpack.

"Hi," she said.

"I was just wondering—there's a football game on Thursday."

"I know," she said.

"I was wondering—are you going?"

"As a matter of fact, I am," she said. She smiled pleasantly at me and closed her locker. "I talked to the janitor like you said," she said. "He fixed my locker door so it doesn't stick anymore." She slung the backpack over one shoulder. She was getting ready to walk away.

"I...I'm glad your locker is working now."

She gave me a funny look. But then she smiled. "Well, see you," she said.

"Yeah. See you."

She walked away. I hated myself as I just stood there in the hall like some kind of statue. Mark would have handled it differently. And if he'd been there watching me, he'd never have let me live down what I'd done. I imagined him shaking his head. I imagined him telling me, "That was pathetic, Jordy. Just pathetic."

Chapter Eight

"It was especially hard," my father reads, "to hear one of the accused tell the court exactly what happened that night."

The prosecution had finished. Now it was time for the defense lawyers to present their cases. My parents talked a lot about whether any of the four defendants would testify.

"They don't have to," my father said. "They probably won't. Why would they?

It's all circumstantial. No one actually saw them beat Mark up. Their lawyers have been trying to make it look like they just came along afterward. They're probably hoping that that's enough reasonable doubt that they'll get off."

We could tell the next day when we got to court that something was going on.

The prosecutor came up to my parents. He said, "Two of them are going to testify."

"Which two?" my father said.

I held my breath.

"Robert Teale and Kyle Mercer," the prosecutor said.

But they didn't testify that day because the other two lawyers had motions they wanted to present to the judge. It took another week before the trial started up again.

Robert Teale was called to testify. Tony stared at him the whole time he talked. So did Joey. Kyle wasn't in court.

"Robert," his lawyer said, "do you know who killed Mark Spencer?"

"It was Tony and Joey," Robert said. "Tony was mad because Shannon was going out with this guy at her new school."

"And what was his name?" the lawyer said.

"Mark Spencer," Robert said. "Tony said he wanted to teach him a lesson."

"What did he mean by that?"

"He wanted to beat the crap out of him," Robert said.

Tony's lawyer objected.

"Can you tell the court in your own words what happened that night?"

"Tony asked Kyle to find out where Mark was going to be that night and—"

"Are you referring to Kyle Mercer?"

"Yes," Robert said. "Kyle knew Mark. They went to the same school, and Kyle lived on the same street as Mark. He found out that Mark was working that night. Tony said we were going to surprise him after work, and Tony was going to make it clear to him that Shannon was off-limits."

"Then what happened?"

Robert shrugged. "We hung out. I smoked up."

"You smoked marijuana?"

"Yeah," Robert said. "Then we went to where Mark was working, and we waited across the street for him to get off work. It was late. Midnight. There was no one around. We saw Mark come out of the restaurant. He went into a sandwich place, and Tony started to get antsy, like he couldn't wait until he finally came out again. But he finally did. We were waiting for him in the parking lot, away from the street. When he came out of the sandwich shop, Kyle went out onto the sidewalk to wait for him."

"You're referring to Kyle Mercer?"

"Yes," Robert said. "Like I said, Kyle knew him. He called to Mark, and Mark went over to him to see what he wanted. Kyle told him he'd found something in the parking lot, and he got Mark to follow him, you know, get him away from the street. Then Tony went up to him and told him to stay away from Shannon."

"What did Mark do?"

"He smiled. He said, 'What are you going to do, Tony? Are you going to hit me like you hit Michael Riordan?' And Tony just went nuts. I guess he realized that the only way Mark would know that is if Shannon told him. I guess he didn't like the idea of Shannon talking to Mark."

Tony's lawyer objected. He said Robert had no way to know what Tony was thinking.

"What did Tony say?" Robert's lawyer said.

"He said, 'Let's get him.' And then he hit him."

"Tony hit Mark?"

"Yeah."

"What did he hit him with?"

"His fist. He punched him in the stomach. Mark doubled over, and Tony grabbed his shirt and pulled him away from the light and shoved him down to the ground. Mark tried to get up, so Tony kicked him. So did Joey. They really started in."

"Started in?" Robert's lawyer said. "What do you mean by that?"

Robert looked out at the people in the court, but he didn't look at my parents.

"They beat up on him," he said.

"Tony Lofredo and Joey Karagiannis and Kyle Mercer?"

Robert shook his head. "Tony and Joey. Kyle didn't touch him. The only thing Kyle did was tell us where he was and get him to come into the parking lot so that no one could see him. Tony and Joey started to beat on him. Tony found some pipe lying on the ground. He picked it up, and he hit Mark with it."

"What about you, Robert? What did you do?"

"I kicked him a couple of times," Robert said. "But that's all. I was pretty wasted. I was out of it. And I didn't have anything against the guy. I sure didn't know what was going to happen. I was just along for the ride, you know?"

It was the other lawyers' turn after that. Tony's lawyer asked Robert why he had decided to testify and what he had been promised. Robert said he hadn't been promised anything. He said he felt bad about what happened. He said he knew he should have stopped Tony and Joey. Tony's lawyer reminded Robert what the pathologist had said—that Mark had died from being kicked in the head with some steel-toed boots. He asked Robert if he wore steel-toed boots.

"Yes," Robert said. "But I didn't kick him in the head."

"How can you be sure?" Tony's lawyer said. "You said you were pretty wasted. Do you always remember exactly what you did when you were wasted?"

"No, but—"

"So how do you know for sure that you didn't kick Mark Spencer in the head? How do you know for sure that it wasn't you who killed him?"

"I didn't kick him in the head," Robert said. "I know I didn't."

"You told the court you were 'wasted.' You admitted to the court that you don't always remember what you do when you're wasted. You admitted that you kicked Mark Spencer. You admitted that you were wearing steel-toed boots—"

"So was Tony."

"So you really can't be sure that it wasn't you, can you, Robert?" Tony's lawyer said.

Robert's lawyer objected.

Kyle was supposed to testify next. I felt sick to my stomach.

Chapter Nine

"It was even harder," my father reads, "to listen to the youngest of the accused. This is a boy who lived a few doors away from us. His parents were our friends. He went to the same school as our sons, Mark and Jordan. When I first learned that he had been arrested, I thought to myself, There, but for the grace of God, goes my Mark or my Jordan."

I couldn't look at Kyle, and I couldn't *not* look at him. I felt numb all over. Kyle was the same age as me. He'd gone to the same elementary school as me and Mark and then the same high school. He'd been in some of my classes for a while, until he started skipping and hanging out with Tony and the rest of them. And now he was going to talk about what he had done.

The prosecutor asked him how he knew Mark.

"He lived on my street," Kyle said.

"Tell us about that night, Kyle," the prosecutor said.

"Well…" Kyle looked over at the far side of the court where his parents were sitting side by side. His mother nodded to him, like she was encouraging him to go ahead and do the right thing.

I felt myself tense up. The right thing was not to have called out to Mark that night. That was the only right thing. But there his mother was, looking at him like he could make up for all that now.

"Tony knew Shannon had started going out with Mark," Kyle said.

"How did he know that?" the prosecutor said.

"I told him."

"How did Tony react when you told him?"

"He said he was going to put an end to it."

"Did he say how he was going to do that?"

"He said he was going to have a talk with Mark. He asked me to find out where Mark hung out so that Tony could have a talk with him in private."

"In private?"

"Where no one would see Tony talking to him," Kyle said.

"And what did you tell Tony?"

"I said okay."

My stomach felt like a knot. I could hardly breathe.

"Then what happened?"

"Mark worked at a fast-food place. Sometimes he worked real late. I told Tony that."

I held my breath as I waited for the prosecutor's next question. But he didn't ask what I thought he would. Instead he said, "What happened that night, Kyle?"

"We got together, Tony and Joey and Robert and me. Robert had been smoking up all day. He was kind of wasted. We went to the restaurant where Mark worked, and we looked inside to make sure he was there. Then we waited. By the time Mark got off work, almost all the stores around there were closed, and there was hardly anyone on the street.

"Mark came out of the restaurant. He went to a sandwich place. Then he started walking to the bus stop. That's when Tony told me to go and get him. So I called to him and told him I'd found something in the parking lot and didn't know what to do."

"What did Mark say?"

"He asked me what I found."

"What did you say?"

"I said it looked like someone was hurt, and I didn't have a cell phone and didn't know what to do. So he came with me to take a look. And that's when Tony started in on him."

The prosecutor asked Kyle to describe as best he could exactly who had done what.

Kyle said pretty much what Robert had said—that Tony had started it by punching Mark and shoving him to the ground, that Tony had hit Mark with a pipe, that Tony and Joey had done most of the punching and kicking and hitting, but that Robert had kicked Mark a couple of times too.

"What about you, Kyle?" the prosecutor said. "Did you hit Mark?"

"No," Kyle said.

"You were there, you lured him to where Tony and the others were, but you didn't hit him, not even once?"

"No."

"Why not?"

Kyle shrugged. "I knew Mark," he said. "He was okay. I didn't want to hurt him."

"Did you try to stop Tony and the others from hurting him?"

Kyle hung his head for a moment. He looked at his mother again. So did I. There were tears in her eyes.

"Tony was my friend," Kyle said at last. "He asked me to help him get Mark alone, so I did."

"Did it occur to you that Tony wanted to hurt Mark physically?"

"Yes," Kyle said. "I knew he was jealous, on account of Shannon. I thought he would throw some punches. But I didn't know he was going to kill Mark. I didn't know that. If I had known that…"

"If you had known, what?" the prosecutor said.

"I don't know," Kyle said. "Maybe I would have tried to stop Tony. But I didn't know. Tony and Joey were beating on Mark. Then, all of a sudden, Tony had a pipe and was smashing Mark over the head with it. At first Mark fought back. But after a while he was just lying there moaning, and Tony was still kicking him. And then someone shouted, and I saw this guy out on the street, near a pizza delivery car. He called out, asked if everything was okay. Then he came across the street and started to come into the parking lot. So we got out of there. Fast."

"Then what happened?"

"We ran for a couple of blocks. Then Tony said we should split up. He said we shouldn't say anything about what happened.

"The next day, when we heard that Mark was dead, Tony said we should get rid of the clothes we were wearing. He said we should just throw them out.

"Joey said what about his boots? He said they cost a lot of money and there was no way he was going to just throw them out. Robert didn't want to get rid of his Docs, either. I don't think Tony wanted to ditch his boots. He said they should just all clean them real good. He said if we all kept our mouths shut, everything would be okay."

Kyle looked at Tony when he said that. He looked like he was mad at Tony because Tony had turned out to be wrong.

If you asked me, the only reason Kyle was up there was that they had been caught. If they hadn't been caught, he wouldn't be telling his story. His mother wouldn't be looking at him with tears in her eyes and a proud look on her face, like her son was different from Tony and Joey, like her son was doing the right thing.

After the other lawyers asked their questions, Kyle was excused. He looked at me as he went back to his seat. He looked at me and nodded, just a little, like he was my friend, like he'd just done me a big favor.

Chapter Ten

"I was glad, at first, when I heard the role that Kyle Mercer played in the death of our son Mark. But bit by bit, as I listened to what he had to say, I grew bitter and vengeful. Even now, as I read this out for your consideration before these young men are sentenced, I find that I have no mercy left in my heart. I find that I am a changed man, and I don't know whether I can ever change back."

The jury was excused to deliberate. My parents and I went outside. My father paced up and down on the sidewalk. My mother asked me if I wanted to go across the street to a coffee shop with her. I said no.

It was a warm day. There were a couple of benches in the little square outside the courthouse. I went and sat down.

My father paced up and down some more. He called to me, "Tell us if anything happens." Then he crossed the street and went into the coffee place where my mother was. They took a seat in the window where they could see me. The prosecutor had told us that if he didn't see us inside when the jury came back, he would send someone outside to find us.

Twenty minutes went by. My parents came out of the coffee shop and crossed the street again.

"We should go back inside," my mother said.

"I'm going to stay out here," I said. "If they come back, let me know."

My parents went inside. I sat on the bench. I knew it was stupid, but I was hoping that Shannon would come back. I knew she couldn't be in court before she testified. You're not allowed to hear what anyone else is saying until after you've given your testimony. But I thought she would come back after that. She didn't. I wondered whether she even thought about Mark anymore. I wondered, if Mark were still alive, would she still be going out with him?

Mark could be funny. My mother said he was charming. Girls liked him, and not just because he was good-looking. Girls were always making eyes at Mark and trying to get his attention.

Sometimes I'd see him in the hall at school or out on the athletic field. I'd see girls making eyes at him. I'd see girls sauntering over to talk to him. I'd see girls buzzing to each other after one of them had caught his attention for a while. They were all excited around Mark. And I would wonder why I couldn't be more like him. Why did I have to be the shy one, the awkward one? Why was I so afraid to talk to girls when Mark could practically do it in his sleep?

After that second time I talked to the new girl, when I asked her if she was going to the football game, Mark walked in on me at home. I was sprawled on the couch in the basement, flipping through channels but not really paying attention to anything that was on.

Mark grabbed the remote out of my hand and flopped down beside me. He had what he called an unwritten rule: when he was in the room, the remote was his. A lot of times we ended up wrestling for it, but that day I just let him take it from me. He could put on the weather channel for all I cared. I was too mad at myself for not taking it one step further with the girl. I shouldn't have just asked her if she was going to the game. I should have asked her if she wanted to go *with me*. But I hadn't done that. I'd been too chicken.

"Hey, Jordy," Mark said. "What's eating you?"

"Nothing."

"Right," Mark said. He flipped through a few channels before he finally settled on a cartoon show. He laughed at something on the screen and then glanced at me when I didn't join in. "Seriously, Jordy," he said. "What's up?"

"It's nothing," I said.

"Hey, I'm your brother. You got a problem, you can always tell me."

Sometimes Mark liked to give me a hard time. He was smarter than me and better looking, and he had way more confidence. Sometimes he treated me like I was ten years younger than him instead of just one. But other times, like when I was having problems with Mom and Dad, he gave me good advice. Or he talked to them for me and got them to ease up a little. Sometimes he helped me with other stuff, stuff I didn't understand at school. And if there was one thing Mark knew, it was girls.

"I want to ask this girl out, but I'm afraid she'll say no," I said finally.

Mark looked surprised. "Girl?" he said. "What girl?"

"She's a new girl. She's in my home-room."

"Yeah? Is she pretty?"

"Yeah," I said. Just thinking about her made me smile. "She's really pretty."

"Is she seeing someone?" Mark said.

"No. Someone told me that she broke up with her boyfriend before she transferred to our school."

"So what's the problem?" Mark said. "Why don't you just ask her out?"

"What if she says no?"

"What if she says yes?"

"What if she laughs at me?"

"What if she doesn't?" Mark said. "And why would she laugh at you anyway? You're a good-looking guy. Maybe not as gorgeous as your big brother, but you'll do."

When I didn't laugh, he said, "Seriously, Jordy. If you like her and you want to be with her, ask her out. The worst thing that could happen is she'll say no. So what? You can't win all the time. But I'll tell you what—for sure you can't win if you don't play. Ask her."

I couldn't sleep that night. I kept going over and over in my mind what I would say and what she would say. What if I couldn't get the words out? What if I started asking her and then her girlfriends showed up? What if she said no—then what would I say? What if she *did* laugh at me?

I saw her the next day at her locker. I told myself I could do it. I sucked in a deep breath. I ran through what I was going to say. I started to walk to her locker.

Her girlfriends showed up, and I chickened out.

I didn't see her for the rest of the day.

"So?" Mark said that night. "Did you ask her?"

I knew he would think I was totally pathetic if I told him I'd chickened out again, so I said yes. He got me in a neck hold and rubbed the top of my head until my hair was matted.

"Way to go, baby brother," he said. "See, I told you it was easy. I knew you could do it. So I guess I'll see you there, huh? You can introduce me to her."

"I thought you were working that day," I said.

"A guy at work has a thing on the weekend and asked me if I would switch with him. I said yes." He grinned at me. "Way to go, Jordan. I'm proud of you."

He actually sounded proud, which made me feel like a total wuss. I promised myself that, no matter what, I would ask her out the next day.

"Jordan!"

I turned and saw my father in the doorway of the courthouse.

"The jury's coming back," he said.

Chapter Eleven

"I told myself that when the jury came back in, that would be the end of it," my father reads. "I told myself that now I would be able to put the whole thing behind me." He looks up. "I don't mean that I would ever forget my son. I don't mean that. But I thought that if justice were done, that would help somehow."

They were all found guilty, but not all of the same thing. Tony and Joey were convicted of second-degree murder. Robert and Kyle were convicted of manslaughter.

A date was set for sentencing. The prosecutor said that we would have a chance to give victim impact statements before the judge decided how much time Tony and Joey would have to serve. Kyle turned and looked at me again that day before he was led out of court with the others.

"Do you want to make a statement?" my mother asked me that night.

"Do I have to?" I said.

"Of course you have to," my father said. "He was your brother. The judge will take into account what we say before he sentences those guys."

I looked at my mother.

"No," she said softly. "You don't have to. You don't have to do anything you don't want to, Jordan. But your father's right. Making a victim impact statement is important. This whole time, ever since Mark died, everyone has seen those four boys, but no one has seen Mark. Everyone has talked about how Mark died and what those four boys did.

But nobody really got to see Mark, what kind of person he was, how important he was to his family. This is our chance to let people see that, to let them know what those boys did when they killed Mark, to get them to understand what a terrible thing it was for the people who loved Mark."

I looked down at the floor. After a while my mother said, "I know how shy you are, Jordan. I also know how much you miss your brother. If you don't want to stand up in front of everyone and talk about it, it's okay. Really."

My father sat at the dining room table that night and wrote out what he wanted to say. My mother curled up on the couch in the living room with a big pad of paper and wrote what she wanted to say. I went up to my room to think.

My mother was right. I was shy. If I were the one who had died, Mark wouldn't have hesitated. He would have made a statement. But Mark was Mark, and I was me. Mark could do a lot of things I couldn't. For example, Mark could ask a girl out and not worry about whether she was going to say no. I couldn't.

I lied to Mark about asking the new girl out. But I had another plan. I decided I would go to the football game anyway. I would look for her when I got there, and if she was alone, I would go and sit with her.

The whole night before the game, I thought about what I would say to her. Maybe I'd ask her if she followed professional football and, if she did, what her favorite team was. Maybe I'd ask her about her old school and about what she thought of my school. When I thought about it, there was always plenty to talk about.

I was nervous when I started around the athletic field to the bleachers. What if she was with a bunch of her new girlfriends? What if—

Then I spotted her. She was halfway up the bleachers, right near the middle. She wasn't with her girlfriends. She was with a guy. She was with Mark. He was saying something to her, and she laughed. She touched his arm. She looked so happy.

Mark spotted me and waved. I saw his eyes looking all around me, like he was looking for the girl I had supposedly asked to the game.

I turned and ran from the field. As I ran, I spotted Kyle. He was sitting near where Mark was.

Mark didn't get home until late. He must have gone out with her after the game. I wondered where they had gone and what they had done. I heard him come up the stairs. He knocked on my door.

"Go away," I said.

Instead he pushed open the door.

"What's the matter with you, Jordy?" he said. "Didn't you see me at the game? I waved to you. I wanted to introduce you to someone."

Right. The girl he was with.

"You saw her, right?" Mark said, beaming at me. "She's really something, huh? Her name is Shannon. She just came up to me and asked me to the game, just like that. I couldn't believe it."

I just lay there on my bed. I didn't say anything.

I was sitting in homeroom the next morning, staring at the back of Shannon's head. Our homeroom teacher was late coming into class, so almost everyone was talking.

One of Shannon's friends said, "I can't believe how lucky you are. Mark Spencer is so hot. Do you have any idea how many girls wish they could go out with him?"

"He's cute," Shannon agreed. "And he's really nice."

"Are you going to go out with him again?"

"Saturday night."

Shannon's friend groaned. "You're so lucky," she said. "Do you know how many girls are ready to claw your eyes out right now because Mark Spencer asked you out instead of them?"

I felt like someone had punched me right in the gut.

"I'm not even sure how it happened," Shannon said. "He just came up to me and started talking. He said something about football, and I heard myself asking him if he was going to the game." She shook her head as if she couldn't believe it. "He said yes, and I asked him if he'd like to go with me."

"Shannon," her friend said, "you are the luckiest girl I know. Tony would go crazy if he knew you were going out with someone else, especially someone like Mark Spencer."

"If Tony knew, if he ever found out, he'd probably try to beat Mark up," Shannon said. "That's why I transferred schools. I thought he was a nice guy, but I was wrong. Tony Lofredo is the craziest guy I know. I'm glad I don't have to see him anymore."

That was the first I ever heard of Tony Lofredo. The first time I saw him was a little over a week later. Mark and Shannon had already gone out a couple of times. I was outside the school, and I saw them come out. Shannon had her arm looped through Mark's arm, and she was laughing at something Mark was saying. Then this guy went up to Shannon. I had never seen him before. He grabbed Shannon by the arm and tried to pull her away from Mark. I heard him yell at her, "Who is that guy? What are you doing with him?"

"Leave me alone, Tony," Shannon said. That's when I realized who he was.

Mark went up to Tony.

"You heard her," he said, nice and calm, like it never even occurred to him to be afraid. "Let go of her. Leave her alone."

Tony turned to Mark. His face was twisted in anger, and I saw his hands curl into fists. I thought he was going to hit Mark, and you know what? I wanted him to. I wanted him to do what I felt like doing every time I saw Mark with Shannon—I wanted him to hurt Mark.

But just then a cop car came down the street. Maybe it was the look on Tony's face that made it slow down. Shannon looked at the cops. Tony turned. When he saw them, he backed down. He looked at Mark, and then he turned and walked away. I wished at the time that he hadn't.

I didn't go straight home after school that day. Instead I went to the park to hang out. I saw Kyle there. He was horsing around with some guys who didn't go to my school. One of them was Tony.

Kyle saw me and pointed to me. He said something to the guys he was with. After a while they split up, and Kyle walked over to where I was standing.

"Hey, Jordan," he said.

"Hey, Kyle."

"How's things?"

I just shrugged. "Are you friends with those guys?"

"Not really," he said. "I sort of know one of them from around, that's all." I didn't believe him. "Why?"

"I was just wondering. You look like you know them."

Kyle studied me for a moment.

"Hey, is Mark at home?" he said. "I promised my mom I'd make an effort at school."

Right. Like he ever cared what his parents thought.

"I know Mark is good at math," he said. "I thought maybe he could help me out. So, you think he's home?"

I thought about the way Tony Lofredo had looked at Mark. I thought about Kyle horsing around with him and those other guys. I thought about Kyle pointing at me. And now here he was, asking me where Mark was.

"He might be," I said. "Unless he's working."

"Where does he work?"

I thought about Tony again. Then I told Kyle where Mark worked.

"Sometimes he has to work late," I said. "Until midnight."

"At a burger joint, huh?" Kyle said. He smiled. "Maybe I should drop by sometime. You think he'd lay out some free food for a neighbor?"

I doubted he would. Mark was totally honest. But I said, "You never know."

"Yeah, maybe I'll drop by sometime," Kyle said. "In the meantime, tell Mark I said hi."

I said I would.

One week later, Mark was dead.

Chapter Twelve

My father read out his victim impact statement. Then my mother read out hers. Then the judge sentenced the guys who killed Mark. Tony and Joey got ten years, but they could be out sooner. Robert got six years. He could also be out sooner.

Kyle got the least amount of time because he didn't actually touch Mark and because he was only fifteen when it happened, although he had been the one to lure Mark into the parking lot and he had known that Tony wanted to get even with Mark.

Then the judge dropped a real bombshell. He said that because Kyle had spent time in custody before the trial, and since he had shown progress in counseling, had cooperated and had shown remorse, he was going to release Kyle into the community, where he would be on probation.

My parents couldn't believe it when they heard that. My mother cried. Kyle's mother hugged Kyle before they took him away to arrange his release. As he left the courtroom, Kyle looked at me and smiled.

It was late at night a couple of weeks after the end of the trial. I was on my way home from work. I got off the bus and was walking toward my street when someone came out of the shadows toward me. It was Kyle.

"You're not supposed to come near me," I said.

It was true. One of the conditions of Kyle's supervision in the community was that he wasn't supposed to have any contact with me or my parents. But here he was.

Kyle looked hurt.

"I'm not going to hurt you," he said. "I just wanted to tell you I'm sorry about what happened. I didn't know Tony was going to do what he did."

"You knew he wanted to get back at Mark for going with Shannon," I said.

Kyle looked at me. "So did you," he said.

I felt my stomach twist.

"I could have said that in the court," Kyle said. "But I didn't. I could have told them how I knew where Mark was that night. But I didn't, because I felt bad about what happened, and I knew you did too. I just wanted to tell you that. I just wanted to say I'm sorry."

He turned and walked away from my street. I watched him go. I wondered who else he had told—or who he might tell sometime in the future.

That night I had a dream. In my dream, I was sitting behind the wheel of my father's car. It was late at night, when everyone was asleep. I was waiting. I waited until I saw Kyle come out of his house. Then I gunned the engine and steered the car straight for Kyle.

I had that dream a lot.

When I heard that Kyle and his parents had moved out west, clear on the other side of the country, I was glad.

But it didn't change anything. It didn't change what I had done. It didn't change that I couldn't tell anyone. And it didn't change that I was afraid that one day Kyle would say something.

I didn't read out a victim impact statement like my mother and father did. But Mark's death affected me. It affected me more than almost anyone will ever know.

Impact is James C. Dekker's second novel in the Orca Soundings series, following *Scum*. James lives in Toronto, Ontario, and has little impact on those around him.

Orca Soundings

Back
Norah McClintock

Bang
Norah McClintock

Battle of the Bands
K.L. Denman

Big Guy
Robin Stevenson

Blue Moon
Marilyn Halvorson

Breathless
Pam Withers

Bull Rider
Marilyn Halvorson

Bull's Eye
Sarah N. Harvey

Charmed
Carrie Mac

Chill
Colin Frizzell

Crush
Carrie Mac

The Darwin Expedition
Diane Tullson

Dead-End Job
Vicki Grant

Death Wind
William Bell

Down
Norah McClintock

Exit Point
Laura Langston

Exposure
Patricia Murdoch

Fastback Beach
Shirlee Smith Matheson

First Time
Meg Tilly

Grind
Eric Walters

The Hemingway Tradition
Kristin Butcher

Hit Squad
James Heneghan

Home Invasion
Monique Polak

House Party
Eric Walters

Orca Soundings

Orca Soundings

www.orcabook.com

Recent Orca Soundings

Scum

978-1-55143-924-2 • $9.95 • PB
978-1-55143-926-6 • $16.95 • LIB

Spiral

978-1-55143-930-3 • $9.95 • PB
978-1-55143-932-7 • $16.95 • LIB

Recent Orca Soundings

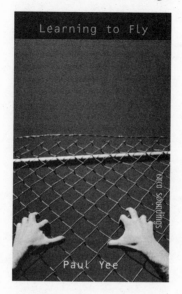

Learning to Fly

978-1-55143-953-2 • $9.95 • PB
978-1-55143-955-6 • $16.95 • LIB

Recent Orca Soundings

First Time

978-1-55143-944-0 • $9.95 • PB
978-1-55143-946-4 • $16.95 • LIB